He Rode That Wave

George Crabb

Leanna,
This was made from my
preaching notes where a
few people gave their lives to
Jesus. God Bless *[signature]*

Going to high school in Santa Cruz, was different than that of any other place. I remember surfing perfect waves was the subject most of us really studied. I remember some days we could hear the waves breaking, smell the salty mist in the air, and school work would just fade away in our thoughts.

So my friends and I would jump on our bikes, leave our high school at lunch recess to check the surf at the point. Sometimes it was so clean and perfect that our school was left behind. You might ask if I regretted doing that. Ah, let me think about that for a moment...NO! The memories of surfing with my friends on hot sunny days in un crowded perfect surf are some of the most treasured memories of my life. It was the closest thing to heaven on earth.

So you can taste, see, smell, and even feel heaven on earth sometimes. Other times it can be hell on earth. War, famine, earthquakes, tsunamis, and disease all reek of death and darkness.

The big wave rider Jay Moriarity was made a legend in the movie "Chasing Mavericks". He was a friend of mine, and I can clearly remember the last time I saw him alive. We were surfing Santa Cruz on a sunny day and I'll never forget how he smiled as I surfed passed him on that warm late afternoon.

Jay was a great big wave rider, but he was just a mortal man like you and me. He rode huge waves, was a good guy, but there was one wave he tragically could not make and that was the wave of death.

The next part of this story is about a Hero who made the drop into this wave of death and He beat it. A friend of His named John penned His words almost 2000 years ago:

For God so loved the world that He gave His only begotten Son, that whoever believes in Him should not parish but have everlasting life.

For God did not send His Son into the world to condemn the world, but that the world through Him might be saved.

(John 3:16,17)

Later John wrote this:

...*If anyone sins, we have an Advocate with the Father, Jesus Christ the righteous. (1ˢᵗ John 2:1)*

We who call Jesus our Lord have got to love that! "Jesus Christ the Righteous", He is our **Advocate, or Lawyer.** Who can possibly accuse us of anything we may have done wrong when we have the greatest Lawyer in the universe. Many may accuse Jesus' people of bad things, but Jesus can reply: "It's OK I've got his back, he's one of mine. He's covered by me, he's my friend, and "I love the Hell out of him".

A story to illustrate this idea of an Advocate, was this team captain I had when I was sponsored by Rip Curl wetsuits - by the way, this was so awesome being sponsored: Two free rip curl wetsuits a month of your choice! Imagine that.

The thing that I loved about this team manager besides the free wetsuits was how he backed his guys. Even when some of us team riders got into trouble he would never give up on us. He kept us on the team if we wanted, no matter how bad we messed up, even when some went to jail. He may have disciplined us but we were still his, still on the team if we wanted to be. He was our advocate or our lawyer, so to speak. So he would keep sponsoring you and continued to give you free gifts even when others would accuse you of being a bad representation of the company, he would keep you on the team.

The Bible also says this about the Son of God:

He Himself is the propitiation for our sins, and not for ours only but also for the whole world. (*1st John 2:2)*

He's the Propitiation for our sins. Propitiation? What the hell is that! Well, Hell is exactly what that is. Propitiation is God's righteous wrath being satisfied. When Jesus hung on that cross He was separated from His Father, God. Separation from God is Hell. God is light and to be separated from Him is to be in the outer darkness away from Him.

Do you remember the movie "Blackhawk down"? It was based on the true story of the Army Rangers, and Delta Force guys in a fierce fire fight that lasted more than eighteen hours in Somalia.

These Rangers were my friends because I was in the same unit called 3rd Ranger Battalion. Though I wasn't there, they told me all about it, sometimes with tears pouring out. Six of my Ranger buddies were killed that day.

It was hell that day! As one of the Blackhawk helicopters was shot out of the sky by a modified RPG, there was just enough guys on the ground to secure the site and rescue the survivors. But suddenly another was brought down in that same way but it crash landed on the other side of the city and no one was able to help the survivor. After that happened all of the birds were ordered to hover to a higher altitude, out of range of the modified rockets.

These Delta Force snipers were in a helicopter witnessing the whole scene. They could clearly see what looked like a cloud of angry, fearless, armed Somalis running for the second crash site.

This crowd had a wrath that had to have blood shed to be satisfied. Some of this wrath was righteous because only days before the US military accidently blew up the wrong buildings with an attack helicopter. Many of those in this crowd found their children, family, and friends dead from this.

So these two Delta operators Gordon, and Randy, asked permission to descend down, to go down to this hell and be dropped off to absorb and fight off this wave of angry, wrath filled Somalis. This was all done so they could save the life of their friend down below.

They knew they were going to die! But they went down because of the love that they had for their friend. After shooting their way to the crash site, they grabbed their injured buddy Mike, hid him away from the crashed helicopter then headed right back to crash site.

They became the focus of the wrathful mob, shooting to their last round. They were then both shot dead, there bodies were cut up, ripped apart and dragged through the streets.

They saved their friend Mike that day, and he is alive and well today, and tears well up every time he tells this story.

Those two heroes became the Propitiation! They satisfied the Mob's wrath with their own blood.

It is also written in Gods word:

For all have sinned and fall short of the glory of God, being justified freely by His grace through the redemption that is in Christ Jesus, whom God set forth as a propitiation by His blood...
(Romans 3:23-25)

So we have all sinned! God hates sin, but not the sinner.

WHAT IS SIN?

Just one example of Sin is Gossip. Have you ever gossiped?

We are all born with a sin nature, but what is it? It is like a worm in an apple.

Did you know worms we may find in a seemingly perfect apple was actually an egg placed in the blossoming flower on the apple tree before it was ever an apple. As it grows and matures the egg hatches inside of the apple and the worm eats its way from the inside out - It bores a hole from inside out.

Or you could say its like a bookworm! It eats up the words, the content or the pages of your life. So this worm we call sin has to be dealt with or it will spread and destroy everything.

The Father has a righteous wrath against that worm we call sin. He hates sin because of what it does to his children. Sin has to be dealt with and we are all born with it.

WHAT DOES OUR WORLD SAY ABOUT SIN?

It doesn't exist! Or, Ignore it! In other words, PLAY DEAD! Really? Just play dead?

I was listening to this Bear Expert talk about what to do if attacked by a bear. Well, he told a story about a time when he was attacked by one up in Alaska. He began to describe how he played dead while the bear began to eat his arm and talked about how it was working well - playing dead while the bear eats you. PLAY DEAD WHILE THE BEAR EATS YOU! REALLY?

Ill tell you what Im going to do. First thing is to pray, simply start talking to Jesus and ask Him to deal with that bear, or sin, because He can stop it.

Then run like hell. Run away from anything that will destroy you.

The wisest man who lived named Solomon, penned this and pictured it well in the proverbs:

Like a roaring lion and a charging bear is a wicked ruler over poor people.

Sin can be this wicked ruler over our lives, ripping us off and making us slaves:

Drinking, drugs, or sex can be that sin.

Maybe your sin is gossip. Do you mock others? This is one of the biggest problems in many church groups today.

So all of this sin in our world feeds this, destructive, massive wave of wrath that none of us are capable of stopping.

Ever notice how waves stand up by an invisible force just under the surface of the water? Our sin in this world is like that, it has been feeding a huge destructive wave.

Remember the giant Tsunamis in Japan? Those dark waves of destruction were unstoppable, and ugly as they dealt a violent death to many people.

So it all seems hopeless, as no one in all the world could ever stop this massive wave of wrath caused by sin.

Oh but there is hope!

In this the love of God was manifested toward us, that God has sent His only begotten Son into the world, that we might live through Him. In this is love, not that we loved God, but that He loved us and sent His Son to be the propitiation for our sins.

(1 John 4:9-10)

Isaiah 53 was penned centuries before Jesus was born. The dead sea scrolls were on display in Seattle and I was actually able to look at this very scripture on a scroll that was penned before Jesus was born. Amazingly the bible today is the same as the ancient scrolls of over 2000 years ago. Lets take a look at this penned by Isaiah over 700 years before Jesus was born:

He is despised and rejected by men, a man of sorrows and acquainted with grief. And we hid as it were, our faces from Him; He was despised, and we did not esteem Him. Surely He has borne our grief's and carried our sorrows; Yet we esteemed Him stricken,

smitten by God, and afflicted. But <u>He was wounded for</u>
<u>our transgressions, He was bruised for our iniquities;</u>
<u>The chastisement for our peace was upon Him, and by</u>
<u>His stripes we are healed.</u> All we like sheep have gone
astray; We have turned, every one, to his own way;
And the Lord has laid on Him the iniquity (sin) of us
all.

Jesus was wounded for our sins! By the sharp whip His
body was broken open, and His blood was poured out, to
heal us! He was nailed to the cross, and the sin of us all
was laid on Him.

Out of love Jesus was sent by the Father to deal with this
Tsunami of wrath fed by our sins.

Mavericks is a hellacious big wave spot. My friends told
me stories of how the wave breaks so hard that you can
feel the ground shake when standing on the cliffs near
by. One of my buddies said he saw rocks explode out of

the white water in the impact zone one time.

I remember getting slammed to the bottom by a huge wave at a famous big wave spot called Steamer Lane in Santa Cruz. It was one of the scariest moments of my life. This monster of a wave pinned me down to the reef, and it was so dark down there that it was black. There was no light and as I swam up it was still turbulent and there was no way to tell which way was up. I almost died.

Out of love Jesus was sent by the father to deal with this Tsunami or wave of wrath fed by our sin. Only Jesus could make the drop down this dark mountainous wave of wrath.

He rode down into the deepest, darkest, thickest, ugliest abyss of a crushing wave imaginable. People who were watching on the cliff were yelling, "why wont He save himself and just kick out of that monster wave."

He was suddenly driven harshly down to the bottom, dragged across the bone yard reef of death causing Him to bleed. He was completely smashed by this wave. This was the wipeout of all time!

When all lost hope, thinking he was swallowed up by the sea, something out of this world happened. Three days later He reappeared, He was resurrected, spit out of that dark abyss of death.

Just like Jonah was spit out of the belly of the fish after three days, so was Jesus spit out of the "Pit" of this wave.

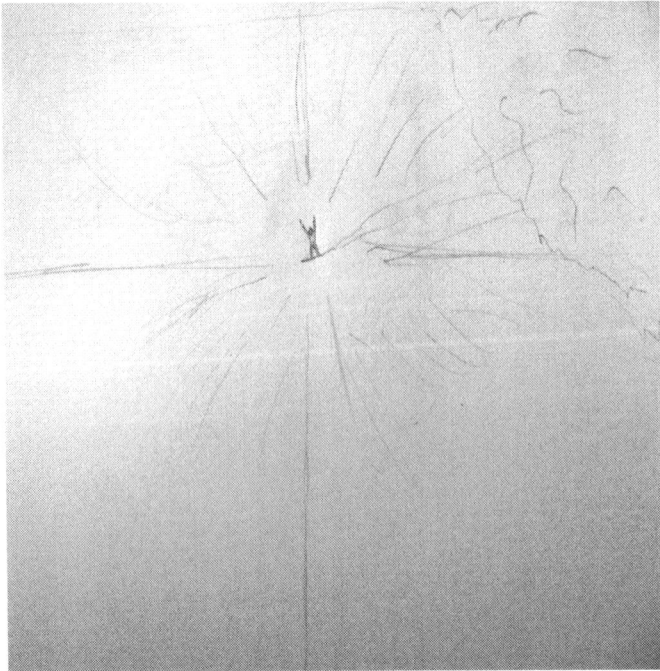

THAT'S IT!   IT IS FINISHED HE BECAME THE
PROPITIATION!

GODS RIGHTEOUS WRATH WAS SATIFIED!

JESUS IS THE WORLD CHAMPION! BECAUSE HE
CONQURED THIS SINFUL WORLD.

Many throughout history were thought to be GREAT!
There was Napoleon the Great, Alexander the Great, or
HEROD THE GREAT.

Really? Herod the Great? The guy who actually tried
to kill baby Jesus, by killing all of the baby boys in that
region 2 years and younger.

So here's the point, its really **"Jesus the Great"**!

The Bible says:

The Lord on high is mightier than the noise of many waters, than the mighty waves of sea. (Psalm 93)

If today you hear His voice, do not harden your heart. (Psalm 95)

The Holy Spirit of God is all around this place and you can feel Him working in your heart right now. But if you harden your heart against the Holy Spirit, you have rejected God.

To reject God is to choose hell.

God is not a dictator! He wants you to choose for yourself to be with Him or against Him.

Some will say: "Why would I follow a God who sends people to hell?"

God is actually giving everyone exactly what they want! Hell is to have a world without God. To be separated from God! That is why hell is described as the "Outer Darkness", because God is light, and if you reject God' then you reject His light.

That light is Jesus and He said:

"I am the Light of the World. He who follows Me shall not walk in darkness, but have the light of life."

All of us in this world are the picture of the two who were crucified with Jesus. We are all dying the day we were born.

Both of the men hanging on their crosses on either side

of Jesus were dying, they both started out mocking Him, but one of them confessed of being a sinner but this Jesus did nothing wrong. Then this guy softened his heart called Jesus Lord and then Jesus said to him **"you will be with me in paradise"**.

That guy was not a good person, and there was not one good work he could have done hanging on that cross. But he was forgiven and given life, forever. Heaven is full of bad people who are simply forgiven. So You can come to Him just as you are, sins and all and He will forgive you, because He loves you.

So to those who believe:

The Holy Spirit is the sweet aroma of life, and the name JESUS is like the sound of living water, a sweet, sweet sound to our ears.

But to those who have harden their hearts and choose not to believe and call Him Lord:

The Holy Spirit is the foul aroma of a dark death, and the name Jesus sounds like the dark, raging wave of God's wrath.

Interesting isn't it! How many people freak out when the name "Jesus" is said as the only way to God. No one cares if you say Buddha, Allah, Mohamed, or You are the only way to God. But if you say "JESUS IS THE ONLY WAY TO GOD" people start tripping, and often get angry. It is because there is power in His name.

There is also Power in His Blood!

Here's a story to illustrate the power of His blood:

When my first born son was around 5 months old, he was dying of a rare disease called "Evens Syndrome".

I was at work and my boss suddenly came up to me and said "Your wife just called from Stanford University

Hospital, she said your son is dying".

My heart sank low, and I began to pray. Arriving at the hospital I saw my son, and he looked pale, yellow, and very lethargic. The doctors told me he had almost no blood cells, but was some how still alive with 100% oxygen to his body.

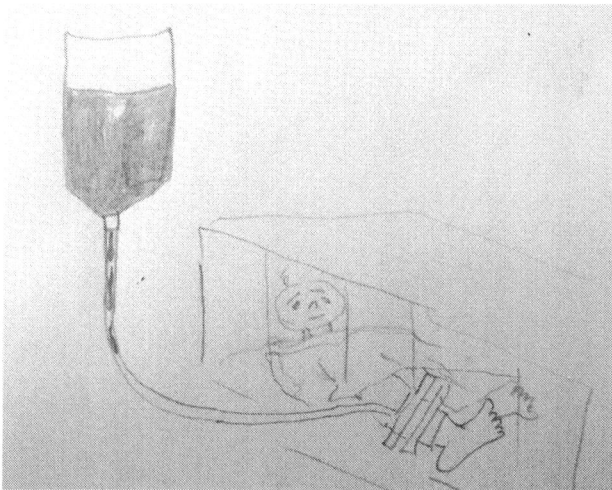

The doctors said his only chance for living was to find a blood match, and to give him a blood transfusion. Finally the blood match came. I watched carefully as the blood dripped down the tube, and into his dying, pale, lifeless body. As soon as it reached him his skin changed from pale yellow, to pink, and his lifeless body came to life. He actually rolled over for the first time, and had a smile from ear to ear.

Now imagine if there was this organic, new pill that came out, that caused you to live forever. This pill puts you in the prime of your life like being in your twenties. You receive a fresh new body, the prime body you always wanted. If you suffer from balding, you even get a full head of real hair.

This pill also gives you peace, a sound mind, patience, wisdom, understanding, and a deep joy in your heart.

This pill comes with the ultimate retirement plan: a paid for condo in the most beautiful city in the world. This city will have a perfect government, excellent community activities, and perfect warm beaches with excellent waves.

The amazing thing is this life saving pill is absolutely free, no charge. Oh, and by the way you can even get high off of this pill with no harm.

Who's taking this free gift? Im taking it! You would be crazy not to take it.

Jesus is the name of this pill, and its made up of His precious blood!

The Center for Disease Control stockpiles huge amounts of vaccines and pills to battle potential disease OUTBREAKS such as the H1N1 virus, or small pocks.

The funny thing is, life on this earth has had this OUTBREAK of the sin virus since the beginning and we are all dying from it. The only medicine, the only vaccination is found in Jesus' precious blood. It was by His bleeding stripes we are healed, and this healing is offered to anyone who asks for it.

There is a sweet song that goes:

What can wash away my sin? Nothing but the blood of Jesus!

This blood of His was shed out of love, for our salvation, freely given to all who ask for it, no charge.

This song illustrates this well:

Thank you Lord, for saving my soul

Thank you Lord, for making me whole

*Thank you Lord, **FORGIVING to Me**, thy great*

salvation so rich and so free.

FORGIVING to ME. Break it down:

FOR	**GIVING**
Forwarding	Salvation
("For" – Golf)	Mercy Grace

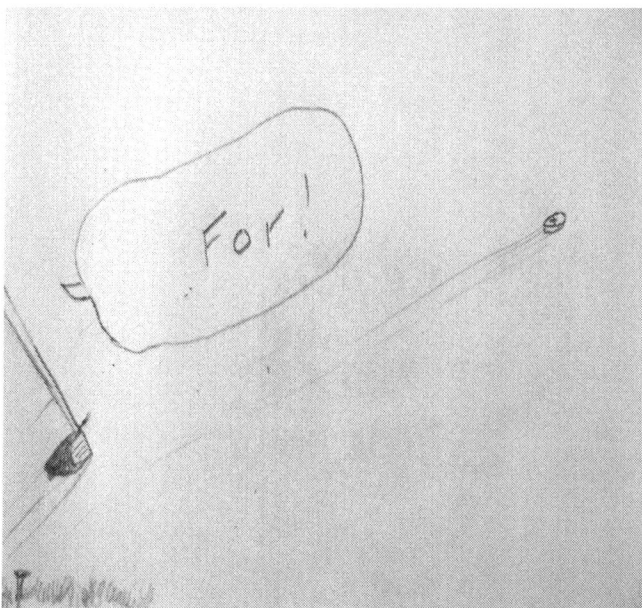

Mercy = not getting the punishment you deserve.

Grace = getting something rich and good that you don't deserve. (like that pill)

This is all about His love for you. Gods love runs deeper than the deepest oceans.

You may be a liberal, a conservative, a progressive, a libertarian, green party, red neck, hippie, gangster it doesn't matter. His LOVE permeates through it all. His love is greater than all governments, and all religions. No one or nothing can stop the love of God, but you! You can reject it by hardening your heart.

You see, God owns it all. He owns Heaven, and Earth. Even the deepest darkest part of hell is in His control and all of hell must bow down to Him.

Right now Jesus is willing to love the hell out of you! Will you allow Him to save you.

So if today you hear His voice, don't harden your heart, it may be your only chance. His voice may be a gentle knock on the door of your heart. Open that door and receive your free gift. Accept Jesus' love into your heart, and live forever and ever. Don't wait until later because your heart may grow thick and closed never to open to Him again. So do it now.

Here's how you can do it:

If you want to receive this gift of life from Jesus, and be saved by Him you can do so today.

You may be hearing this for your first time or you may have gone to church all your life and even call yourself a Christian. Either way you know that have never had a relationship with Jesus, but now you want to believe in Him and have this relationship with Him. If this speaks of you and you want to belong to Jesus then you can repeat this simple prayer after me and receive Jesus into your heart:

"O God, I am a sinner. I am sorry for my sin. Forgive me. I want to turn from my sin. I receive Jesus as my Savior; I confess Him as my Lord. From now on I want to follow Him. In Jesus' Name. Amen."

Now may the Holy Spirit fill you up just as a spring overflows with living water.

Now make sure you go to a Bible teaching church like this one, and go in the peace and blessing of God, through Jesus our Lord.

Notes

Made in the USA
Charleston, SC
15 October 2013